ADVENT OF
THE SAVIOR

6 STUDIES FOR INDIVIDUALS OR GROUPS

LifeGuide®
BIBLE STUDIES

CINDY BUNCH, EDITOR

IVP Connect

An imprint of InterVarsity Press
Downers Grove, Illinois

InterVarsity Press
P.O. Box 1400, Downers Grove, IL 60515-1426
www.ivpress.com
email@ivpress.com

©2009 by InterVarsity Christian Fellowship/USA

InterVarsity Press® is the book-publishing division of InterVarsity Christian Fellowship/USA®, a movement of students and faculty active on campus at hundreds of universities, colleges and schools of nursing in the United States of America, and a member movement of the International Fellowship of Evangelical Students. For information about local and regional activities, visit intervarsity.org.

LifeGuide® is a registered trademark of InterVarsity Christian Fellowship.

All Scripture quotations, unless otherwise indicated, are taken from the Holy Bible, New International Version®. NIV®. Copyright ©1973, 1978, 1984 by International Bible Society. Used by permission of Zondervan Publishing House. All rights reserved.

See also the sources at the back of the guide.

Cover image: © Jill Ferry / Trevillion Images

ISBN 978-0-8308-3136-4

Printed in the United States of America ∞

 As a member of the Green Press Initiative, InterVarsity Press is committed to protecting the environment and to the responsible use of natural resources. To learn more, visit greenpressinitiative.org.

| P | 25 | 24 | 23 | 22 | 21 | 20 | 19 |
| Y | 30 | 29 | 28 | 27 | 26 | 25 | 24 |

Contents

Getting the Most Out of
Advent of the Savior

Two years ago I made plans to go on a silent Advent retreat with my mother. I had been attending the overnight retreats sponsored by Karen Mains's Hungry Souls ministry for several years. They take place midweek in the first week of December. It's hard to think of going away at such a busy time of year, but I had found these retreats to be a beautiful way to focus my thoughts on Christ during the season ahead. This year I'd invited my mother to fly in to join me.

When I walked out of the house to put a suitcase in the car, our nine-month-old puppy followed me. He decided to make a break for it, dashing out the garage door and around the corner toward the local restaurants and shops with me chasing him about a half block behind. I watched in horror as he ran into the street, straight into the wheel of a car. He was thrown back onto the snowy, wet curb and was in a snarling lump when I reached him.

I got him back home and wrapped him up in towels just as my mother arrived at my house ready for our contemplative retreat. I, however, was not exactly in a peaceful frame of mind. Instead I was wondering if our puppy had any broken bones and whether we should take him to the vet, and at the same time was feeling angry at his bad behavior (not the first such offense!).

This is the stuff of real-life spirituality. As we try to make space for God, our devotion is interrupted by the world around us as life presses in. Yet, a $325 x-ray determined that my dog was actually fine—just bruised—and so my mother and I did have an opportunity to open our hearts for the coming of Christ.

The weeks preceding Christmas can be one of the most difficult times for us to focus on God. We feel the weight of buying gifts, preparing for guests, putting up the Christmas tree and stringing the lights, baking cookies and fitting in parties all alongside our regular work lives. Sometimes it feels more like work than celebration.

It takes great intentionality to make space for Christ during the Christmas season. Maybe that's why the Scriptures offer so many angles from which to view the birth of Christ—the perspectives of his parents, his aunt and uncle, shepherds doing a day's work, far-off Magi and nearby despots—even the perspective of the prophets who preceded him by centuries. These Bible studies take up each of those perspectives in the hopes that you will get a fresh vision of the coming Christ.

When we allow ourselves to enter into it, Scripture reminds us that Christmas is not a task to be done but a celebration to be marveled at.

The Season of Advent

This guide has been compiled from LifeGuide® Bible studies with an eye toward helping groups and individuals to prepare for Christmas. The season of Advent begins on the Sunday directly following Thanksgiving and continues for a total of four Sundays. Christmas day is then celebrated as a separate "week" in liturgical tradition.

Epiphany* is the celebration of the coming of the Magi. The Feast of the Epiphany is January 6. Many Protestant churches then regard the following five to nine weeks (depending on the

---

*Information on the seasons taken from *Living the Christian Year* by Bobby Gross (Downers Grove, Ill.: IVP Books, 2009). The baptism of Jesus is celebrated the week after the Feast of the Epiphany. He also notes, "In the Roman Catholic and much of the Anglican tradition, the period after the Baptism of the Lord is designated as either Ordinary Time or simply the Season after Epiphany."

date of Easter for that year) as the season of Epiphany. Epiphany ends with Ash Wednesday and the beginning of Lent.

As you think about how to cover this material in six weeks, I would suggest beginning the week before Thanksgiving with study one, Isaiah's prophecy, and concluding with the sixth study on the Magi in the week after Christmas. You might want to celebrate the Feast of the Epiphany as a group to conclude your study.

If you aren't able to cover all the studies during Advent, you can continue into the Epiphany season, a very appropriate time in which to ponder the birth of Jesus. You might also want to pick three or four of the studies and cover them during this Advent season and continue with the rest of them next year.

Meeting Christ in the Season of Advent

Below are some ideas adapted from *Living the Christian Year* by Bobby Gross for meeting Christ during the seasons of Advent and Epiphany. Pick just one or two that are realistic for your life and an encouragement to you.

- Spend some time in silence rereading the Christmas narrative in the Gospels—whether for two hours or a day of retreat.

- Emphasize Christmas decorations that remind you of Christ, such as manger scenes.

- Get outdoors to enjoy the creation hallowed by Christ's incarnation.

- Buy or make an Advent wreath and light the appropriate candle(s) at dinner each night.

- Light a candle and sit in silence for five minutes each day. Sit somewhere that allows you to enjoy your Christmas tree or a manger scene.

- Participate in an opportunity to give to someone in need through church or school.

- Plan one or two special activities to do with your children or your friends—such as a concert or a play.

- Keep your tree and decorations up until the end of the season on January 6.

- Host a leftovers party on December 26 for friends or neighbors.

- Save some of your gift-giving for the twelve days of Christmas, especially, perhaps, for the Feast of the Epiphany.

- Hold a Twelfth Night party on the eve of Epiphany.

May this Advent be one in which you are blessed with a renewed sense of the miracle of Christmas in the coming of the Savior.

Suggestions for Individual Study

1. As you begin each study, pray that God will speak to you through his Word.

2. Read the introduction to the study and respond to the personal reflection question or exercise. This is designed to help you focus on God and on the theme of the study.

3. Each study deals with a particular passage so that you can delve into the author's meaning in that context. Read and reread the passage to be studied. The questions are written using the language of the New International Version, so you may wish to use that version of the Bible. The New Revised Standard Version is also recommended.

4. This is an inductive Bible study, designed to help you discover for yourself what Scripture is saying. The study includes three types of questions. *Observation* questions ask about the basic facts: who, what, when, where and how. *Interpretation* questions delve into the meaning of the passage. *Application* questions help you discover the implications of the text for growing in Christ. These three keys unlock the treasures of Scripture.

Write your answers to the questions in the spaces provided or in a personal journal. Writing can bring clarity and deeper understanding of yourself and of God's Word.

5. It might be good to have a Bible dictionary handy. Use it to look up any unfamiliar words, names or places.

6. Use the prayer suggestion to guide you in thanking God for what you have learned and to pray about the applications that have come to mind.

7. You may want to go on to the suggestion under "Now or Later," or you may want to use that idea for your next study.

Suggestions for Members of a Group Study

1. Come to the study prepared. Follow the suggestions for individual study mentioned above. You will find that careful preparation will greatly enrich your time spent in group discussion.

2. Be willing to participate in the discussion. The leader of your group will not be lecturing. Instead, he or she will be encouraging the members of the group to discuss what they have learned. The leader will be asking the questions that are found in this guide.

3. Stick to the topic being discussed. Your answers should be based on the verses which are the focus of the discussion and not on outside authorities such as commentaries or speakers. These studies focus on a particular passage of Scripture. Only rarely should you refer to other portions of the Bible. This allows for everyone to participate in in-depth study on equal ground.

4. Be sensitive to the other members of the group. Listen attentively when they describe what they have learned. You may be surprised by their insights! Each question assumes a variety of answers. Many questions do not have "right" answers, particularly questions that aim at meaning or application. Instead the questions push us to explore the passage more thoroughly.

When possible, link what you say to the comments of others. Also, be affirming whenever you can. This will encourage some of the more hesitant members of the group to participate.

5. Be careful not to dominate the discussion. We are sometimes so eager to express our thoughts that we leave too little opportunity for others to respond. By all means participate! But allow others to also.

6. Expect God to teach you through the passage being discussed and through the other members of the group. Pray that you will have an enjoyable and profitable time together, but also that as a result of the study you will find ways that you can take action individually and/or as a group.

7. Remember that anything said in the group is considered confidential and should not be discussed outside the group unless specific permission is given to do so.

8. If you are the group leader, you will find additional suggestions at the back of the guide.

1

To Us a Child Is Born

Isaiah's Prophecy

Isaiah 9:1-7

Christmas is heralded as a time of joy, friendship and celebration. But the reality is that it is not always a happy season. As I write, this Advent a dear friend sits at the side of his forty-five-year-old wife who just this week has learned she has terminal cancer. Christmas can remind us of past losses, the family we wish we had or our economic stress.

GROUP DISCUSSION. How are you approaching this season this year? Do you feel pressure to put on a false face or do you feel ready to dive in?

PERSONAL REFLECTION. Talk with God about how you are feeling as you approach Christmas. If you are feeling frustration or disappointment, express your feelings. Allow yourself to sit in his presence for a few moments and listen for his response.

As we turn to this beautiful passage of Isaiah, memorably recorded in Handel's *Messiah,* we encounter the people of Israel and Judah in a terrible state. King Ahaz has turned away from the sign God offered him, but now Isaiah prophesies of a greater King who is coming to put things right. *Read Isaiah 9:1-7.*

---

1. With the help of the map find the regions of Zebulun, Naphtali and Galilee and the road called "the Way of the Sea." This road marked the western limits of Palestine and the Jordan marked the eastern limits.

2. Describe a time when you have been overwhelmed with the reality of the darkness and evil which is present in our world.

_____

3. The light dawns in verses 2-5. What specific changes does Isaiah predict?

_____

4. Look at Isaiah 8:19-22. What do you learn about the state of mind of the people from these verses?

_____

5. What do you think it would have been like for the people to hear Isaiah's words in 9:2-5?

_____

6. How has the Lord brought light into your dark corner of the world?

7. Verses 2-5 are the trumpet fanfare announcing the arrival of the new ruler. Verse 4 refers to the military hero Gideon defeating Midian. But what is this new ruler like according to verses 6-7?

8. Reflect on the names in verse 6. What significance does each one have?

9. In what ways is the coming of the kingdom of justice and righteousness mentioned in verse 7 good news for the poor, the needy and the oppressed?

10. Which of these titles—"Wonderful Counselor, Mighty God, Everlasting Father, Prince of Peace"—particularly describes God as you have known him during a time of difficulty?

11. As you approach Advent, which of these aspects would you particularly like to experience and why?

---

12. What would you like to do in the approaching weeks of Advent to focus your mind and heart on Christ? (See "Getting the Most Out of *Advent of the Savior*" for a list of ideas.)

Ask God to prepare your heart for the coming of Christ.

Now or Later

In the next studies we will see many responses of worship both to the announcement of Jesus and to his birth. In the book of Revelation, worshiping the Lamb on the throne is the central activity of heaven. Revelation completes the story of Jesus coming to earth. Read Revelation 4—5 for a beautiful picture of eternal worship.

2

Waiting and Hoping

Zechariah and the Angel

Luke 1:1-25; 57-80

The couple in California made front-page news. They were in their mid-sixties, and she was expecting their first child! A week later a photo of the fine-looking immigrant couple from the Philippines and their beautiful baby daughter was released. After forty years their dreams came true.

GROUP DISCUSSION. What thoughts rush into your mind as you consider the story of the California couple?

PERSONAL REFLECTION. Think of an extraordinary personal experience that you could not account for apart from God's unique intervention. What bigger view of God did you learn from that?

Luke begins his Gospel with a similar sensational event—a couple past their reproductive years also having their first child. But the country into which their son was born was very different from affluent America. Israel was a small, second-rate country occupied by imperial Rome. It is 4 B.C. The people had not heard from God in over four hundred years and were starting to wonder if God had forgotten them. Had he reneged on his many promises to send Messiah to deliver them? *Read Luke 1:1-25.*

1. What do you learn about Luke's reasons for writing and his approach from verses 1-4?

2. Verse 7 tells us that Zechariah and Elizabeth were both barren and aging. What do you think this experience would have been like for them—especially in a culture in which parents and children worked together in a trade or in the fields?

3. God chose this elderly couple for an extraordinary job. Several factors in verses 5-10 give hints of God's reasons for this choice. What might those reasons be?

4. From what you read throughout these verses, how would you describe the angel who appears to Zechariah?

How is this depiction of an angel similar to or different from the ways in which you've seen angels depicted in the media or art?

---

5. Do you find yourself sympathetic or critical of Zechariah's response of unbelief (vv. 18-22)? Explain your view.

---

6. How do the people respond to Zechariah when he emerges (vv. 21-22)?

---

7. Note Elizabeth's response (vv. 24-25). What kinds of emotions do you think she was having during this time?

8. *Read Luke 1:57-80.* At what point was Zechariah able to speak again (vv. 59-62)?

---

9. Note that Luke describes people's spontaneous reactions to John's birth three times. What might be Luke's purpose in repeating this fact?

---

10. The Holy Spirit sharpened Zechariah's faith to see (1) the great acts that God's Redeemer will do (vv. 68-75) and (2) his child's unique relation to this Redeemer (vv. 76-79). Suppose you were one of the neighbors listening to his prophecy. As a devout Jew, which part would have especially stirred you?

---

11. Reflect on the kind of God you have seen in this chapter. What is this God telling you about how to approach a discouraging situation that you are facing or that you see in the world?

Thank God for being the only source of true hope.

Now or Later

The Advent stories may lead you to want to inquire more about angels. The following passages will give you a good starting place. Hebrews 1 gives an overall understanding of angels to people who then were tempted to worship them (see especially verse 14). Angels were active throughout the Old Testament. They witnessed creation (Job 38:7), destroyed evildoers (Genesis 19:1ff.), have warlike potential (Genesis 32:1-22), restrained a false prophet (Numbers 22:21-35), mediated God's law to Moses (Acts 7:38, 53), served as God's messengers (Judges 6:11-23), aided his servants (1 Kings 19:5-7) and gave military assistance (2 Kings 19:35). They also strengthened Jesus in temptation (Mark 1:13; Luke 22:43) and were present at his resurrection and ascension (Luke 24:4-7; Acts 1:9-11). They guided the apostles in evangelization as well (Acts 8:26; 10:3-8; 12:7-10; 27:23).

3

Nothing Is Impossible

Mary and the Angel

At the beginning of an Advent retreat I attended, a wonderful painting was displayed at the front of the room: *The Annunciation* by Fra Angelico.* Our retreat leaders invited us all to come look at it and then began a discussion centered on the painting. They encouraged us to notice the humble posture of Mary and the powerful presence of the angel. We also discussed the background imagery of creation, showing Adam and Eve in the Garden. But I found myself most captivated by Mary's blue robe that symbolizes royalty and surrounds her dress of pale red, which symbolizes her human nature. God was draping Mary in his kingly glory. And she gracefully accepted her calling.

GROUP DISCUSSION. Describe a time in your experience, or in the experience of someone you know, when life's direction was changed by one event or decision.

---

*You can view the *The Annunciation* altarpiece at the Museo Nacional del Prado: <http://www.museodelprado.es/en/ingles/collection/on-line-gallery/on-line-gallery/obra/the-annunciation-7/>.

PERSONAL REFLECTION. "All of you who were baptized into Christ have clothed yourselves with Christ" (Galatians 3:27). Picture yourself draped in God's glorious robes of blue. What thoughts and feelings do you have?

When Mary met the angel she was probably about fourteen years old, as that is when betrothal and marriage took place at that time. *Read Luke 1:26-38.*

1. This passage chronicles some amazing events. What words and phrases give you an idea of what this experience was like for Mary?

2. The angel referred to Mary twice as "favored" by God (vv. 28, 30). The word is based on the Greek word for "grace." What insight does that give you into why God chose Mary to give birth to Jesus?

3. Sit with the word "favored" for a moment. What would it be like to hear God call you "highly favored"?

4. What specific information does the angel Gabriel give to Mary about the son she would bear (vv. 31-33, 35)?

---

5. Mary responds to the angel's declaration by asking how the promise would be fulfilled (v. 34). Do you think Mary's question was an expression of doubt? Explain.

---

6. What do you think would have been your response to a call from God for such a sacrifice on your part?

---

7. *Read Luke 1:39-45.* In what way would the information given by the Holy Spirit to Elizabeth encourage Mary and strengthen her faith?

---

8. Read Luke 1:46-56. What aspects of God's character are mentioned in Mary's praise to God?

9. How does Mary describe herself in her poem to God?

_____

10. In this passage we've seen Mary's faith in God, her humble servantlike attitude, and her personal knowledge of the character of God. Which of these traits in Mary are you most drawn to? Why?

_____

11. Verse 37 says, "Nothing is impossible with God." In what area of your life do you need to embrace this teaching?

Ask God to build in you an attitude of humility and gratefulness like Mary.

Now or Later

As you reflect on God's goodness to you, you may want to write a song or poem or letter to God that expresses your joy in him. Then pray or sing or read what you have written. Share your "hymn" with your group or with a Christian friend.

4

Divine Interruption

Joseph and the Angel

Matthew 1:18-25

In his dramatic retelling of Scripture, *The Book of God,* Walter Wangerin imagines the conversation Joseph might have had with Mary's worried father and then with Mary.

Pale in the interior dark—scarcely visible, as if she were winter's breath on the air—Mary was gazing out at Joseph, hesitating, chewing her bottom lip. Oh, the worry on her features broke his heart!

Joseph couldn't help himself: he ran past Joachim and gathered Mary into his arms and held her tightly to his body.

"I love you," he whispered in her tender ear. "Don't cry, don't cry. I love you, Mary, and I know who is sleeping in you, and I will love him, too. It is well. All is well. I know what God is doing, and I love you."*

---

*Walter Wangerin, *The Book of God* (Grand Rapids: Zondervan, 1996), p. 438.

Joseph's relationship with Mary and their marriage plans were interrupted in a most shocking way, and yet he was able to offer her grace.

GROUP DISCUSSION. Think about what it's like to get caught up in someone else's difficult circumstances—with the person perhaps needing more from you than you had expected to give. How do you normally respond to life's interruptions?

PERSONAL REFLECTION. When have you been impatient with an interruption recently—perhaps a small request? Reflect on your response before God.

When Joseph learned that Mary was pregnant, he thought he had only two options—to publicly disgrace the woman he loved or to end their relationship in a private divorce. God's intervention, however, opened up a whole new option that he had never considered. *Read Matthew 1:18-25.*

_____

1. What feelings would you struggle with if you were Joseph on hearing this news?

_____

2. What does Joseph's decision in verse 19 tell you about what kind of man he was?

3. How do you think a typical church might have handled this situation?

4. What important facts does Joseph learn from the angel in the dream (vv. 20-21)?

5. Why do you think God let Joseph work through the struggle of that difficult decision before revealing the true story of Mary's child to him?

6. How did Joseph know that this was a genuine encounter with an angel and not a case of wishful thinking on his part?

7. What confirmation about Mary's character do you find in this passage?

8. What do you think Joseph said to his family after his encounter with the angel?

_____

9. What specific truths can you learn about who Jesus was and what he came to do from the angel's words (vv. 20-21) and from Matthew's reference to Old Testament prophecy (vv. 22-23)?

_____

10. What qualities do you see demonstrated in Joseph's life that would have equipped him to be a good husband to Mary and a godly model to Jesus?

_____

11. What principles can you learn from this passage that will prepare you for the next divine interruption in your own life?

Pray that God will shape in you a spirit that's open to his interruptions.

Now or Later

Keep a list or journal of some of the interruptions you experience this week—from phone calls to larger requests from friends or family. Look for moments of grace and ways God might use those interruptions.

5

Season of Wonder

Jesus' Birth

Luke 2:1-20

Waking Christmas morning and knowing that the magic day has come. Running downstairs to discover what's under the tree. Opening a package and finding something special that was selected just for you. Christmas is a day of delights that we can always approach with fresh wonder.

GROUP DISCUSSION. What do you like best about the way you currently celebrate Christmas?

PERSONAL REFLECTION. You may or may not have had idyllic Christmases as a child, but as you think back over your past Christmases, what are you thankful for?

Try to read and reflect on Luke 2 as though for the first time, looking at the unfolding scenes through the wonder-filled eyes of a child. *Read Luke 2:1-20.*

1. The distance from Nazareth to Bethlehem was about 70 miles. What would it be like to be Joseph taking that weeklong walk from Nazareth to Bethlehem?

What would it be like for Mary?

---

2. If you were in Mary and Joseph's place, what kinds of conversations with God might you be having during this time?

---

3. Luke's account of Jesus' birth reads like a newspaper article (vv. 4-7). What key facts do you learn?

What overall impression does Luke leave you with?

4. What, for you, is the significance of the place and circumstances around Jesus' birth?

_____

5. We like to see shepherds on Christmas cards or in a children's pageant. But back then they were an outcast group. So, what in the angel's message would be incredible to them (vv. 9-14)?

_____

6. What do you notice about the shepherds' response to what they experience (vv. 16-20)?

_____

7. God had been preparing the characters of Mary and Joseph to be Jesus' earthly parents. From all that you have seen of them so far, what qualities of strong character do you perceive?

_____

8. What aspects of their character would you like to emulate and why?

9. We see in the passage how the shepherds rush off to share the good news and then how others respond with amazement. What can you do to nurture the experience of the holy wonder of Christmas for your friends and family?

Ask God to re-create in you a childlike wonder as you ponder the miracle of his Son's birth.

Now or Later

Read Luke 2:21-52 for a number of important events from Jesus' early life.

6

In Search of the King

The Magi Meet Jesus

Matthew 2:1-18

I like to do lots of research when I'm planning a trip. I talk to people, read guidebooks, search the Internet and so on. For me, all of that research feeds into the anticipation of the trip itself; preparation helps me enjoy the journey and enhances my learning. But sometimes a guidebook overstates the beauty or intrigue of a particular spot, and I experience some disappointment with the reality of the trip.

GROUP DISCUSSION. Describe something you once strongly desired (for example, a car, television, stereo or a relationship with a particular person). When you got it, did it fulfill your expectations? Explain why or why not.

PERSONAL REFLECTION. What are you currently waiting for or anticipating? How does it affect your thoughts during the day?

The nation of Israel waited for centuries for God's anointed king to be born. Jesus' birth, however, was not greeted with royal gladness by the nation and its leaders. Instead, there was intrigue and conflict. The political and religious establishment felt threatened by the coming of the Messiah. It was left to foreign leaders to welcome the newborn king. *Read Matthew 2:1-18.*

1. Compare and contrast Jesus the heavenly king and Herod the earthly king in this chapter.

2. There are many traditions and myths in church history about the Magi that may or may not be true. But drawing only from the information in this passage, what can we discover about them?

3. Describe the details of their search for Jesus.

4. How has knowing Jesus involved you in a search or journey—either initially or in your ongoing spiritual life?

5. How has what you have found in your journey with Jesus been similar to or different from what you expected?

6. Compare and contrast the response of the religious leaders (vv. 4-6) to the response of the Magi (vv. 7-12)).

7. On hearing of Jesus' birth from the searching Magi, Herod also begins a search for the newborn Christ (vv. 13-16). How does his search compare with that of the Magi?

8. The responses of the Magi and Herod are typical of the ways people respond to Jesus today. Describe some different responses to Jesus you have witnessed?

What factors might cause people to respond to Jesus in radically different ways?

9. God is the unseen actor throughout the chapter. In what ways can we see his behind-the-scenes actions (vv. 6, 15)?

---

10. You may be reading this during a season of Advent or after it. The way in which we celebrate the Christmas season can lead to much anticipation and at times great disappointment. What disappointments has the most recent season brought for you?

What gifts has it brought?

---

11. What activities or practices might help you to foster a season of Advent which is centered on the Christ child who has come to fulfill God's promises to us?

Spend time worshiping the King of kings. Then ask God to help you tell others about him.

Now or Later

The Feast of the Epiphany is celebrated on January 6. You might want to have a celebration with your group as you conclude your study. One fun way to celebrate is to follow the European and Hispanic tradition of making or purchasing (from a Mexican bakery, for example) an Epiphany bread called Three Kings Cake. Beliefnet.com has recipes for a French, German, Spanish or Mexican king's cake.

The week after Epiphany, Jesus' baptism is commemorated. In the accounts in Mark we see Isaiah's prophecy leading to John's desert preaching and then Jesus' baptism (Mark 1:1-13), weaving together several themes from these studies. See also John 1:1-34.

Leader's Notes

MY GRACE IS SUFFICIENT FOR YOU. *(2 COR 12:9)*

Leading a Bible discussion can be an enjoyable and rewarding experience. But it can also be *scary*—especially if you've never done it before. If this is your feeling, you're in good company. When God asked Moses to lead the Israelites out of Egypt, he replied, "O Lord, please send someone else to do it!" (Ex 4:13). It was the same with Solomon, Jeremiah and Timothy, but God helped these people in spite of their weaknesses, and he will help you as well.

You don't need to be an expert on the Bible or a trained teacher to lead a Bible discussion. The idea behind these inductive studies is that the leader guides group members to discover for themselves what the Bible has to say. This method of learning will allow group members to remember much more of what is said than a lecture would.

These studies are designed to be led easily. As a matter of fact, the flow of questions through the passage from observation to interpretation to application is so natural that you may feel that the studies lead themselves. This study guide is also flexible. You can use it with a variety of groups—student, professional, neighborhood or church groups. Each study takes forty-five to sixty minutes in a group setting.

There are some important facts to know about group dynamics and encouraging discussion. The suggestions listed below should enable you to effectively and enjoyably fulfill your role as leader.

Preparing for the Study

1. Ask God to help you understand and apply the passage in your own life. Unless this happens, you will not be prepared to lead others. Pray too for the various members of the group. Ask God to open your hearts to the message of his Word and motivate you to action.

2. Read the introduction to the entire guide to get an overview of the entire book and the issues which will be explored.

3. As you begin each study, read and reread the assigned Bible passage to familiarize yourself with it.

4. This study guide is based on the New International Version of the Bible. It will help you and the group if you use this translation as the basis for your study and discussion.

5. Carefully work through each question in the study. Spend time in meditation and reflection as you consider how to respond.

6. Write your thoughts and responses in the space provided in the study guide. This will help you to express your understanding of the passage clearly.

7. It might help to have a Bible dictionary handy. Use it to look up any unfamiliar words, names or places. (For additional help on how to study a passage, see chapter five of *How to Lead a LifeGuide Bible Study,* InterVarsity Press.)

8. Consider how you can apply the Scripture to your life. Remember that the group will follow your lead in responding to the studies. They will not go any deeper than you do.

9. Once you have finished your own study of the passage, familiarize yourself with the leader's notes for the study you are leading. These are designed to help you in several ways. First, they tell you the purpose the study guide author had in mind when writing the study. Take time to think through how the

study questions work together to accomplish that purpose. Second, the notes provide you with additional background information or suggestions on group dynamics for various questions. This information can be useful when people have difficulty understanding or answering a question. Third, the leader's notes can alert you to potential problems you may encounter during the study.

10. If you wish to remind yourself of anything mentioned in the leader's notes, make a note to yourself below that question in the study.

Leading the Study

1. Begin the study on time. Open with prayer, asking God to help the group to understand and apply the passage.

2. Be sure that everyone in your group has a study guide. Encourage the group to prepare beforehand for each discussion by reading the introduction to the guide and by working through the questions in the study.

3. At the beginning of your first time together, explain that these studies are meant to be discussions, not lectures. Encourage the members of the group to participate. However, do not put pressure on those who may be hesitant to speak during the first few sessions. You may want to suggest the following guidelines to your group.

☐ Stick to the topic being discussed.

☐ Your responses should be based on the verses which are the focus of the discussion and not on outside authorities such as commentaries or speakers.

☐ These studies focus on a particular passage of Scripture. Only rarely should you refer to other portions of the Bible. This allows for everyone to participate in in-depth study on equal ground.

☐ Anything said in the group is considered confidential and will not be discussed outside the group unless specific permission is given to do so.

□ We will listen attentively to each other and provide time for each person present to talk.

□ We will pray for each other.

4. Have a group member read the introduction at the beginning of the discussion.

5. Every session begins with a group discussion question. The question or activity is meant to be used before the passage is read. The question introduces the theme of the study and encourages group members to begin to open up. Encourage as many members as possible to participate, and be ready to get the discussion going with your own response.

This section is designed to reveal where our thoughts or feelings need to be transformed by Scripture. That is why it is especially important not to read the passage before the discussion question is asked. The passage will tend to color the honest reactions people would otherwise give because they are, of course, supposed to think the way the Bible does.

You may want to supplement the group discussion question with an icebreaker to help people to get comfortable. See the community section of *Small Group Idea Book* for more ideas.

You also might want to use the personal reflection question with your group. Either allow a time of silence for people to respond individually or discuss it together.

6. Have a group member (or members if the passage is long) read aloud the passage to be studied. Then give people several minutes to read the passage again silently so that they can take it all in.

7. Question 1 will generally be an overview question designed to briefly survey the passage. Encourage the group to look at the whole passage, but try to avoid getting sidetracked by questions or issues that will be addressed later in the study.

8. As you ask the questions, keep in mind that they are designed to be used just as they are written. You may simply read

them aloud. Or you may prefer to express them in your own words.

There may be times when it is appropriate to deviate from the study guide. For example, a question may have already been answered. If so, move on to the next question. Or someone may raise an important question not covered in the guide. Take time to discuss it, but try to keep the group from going off on tangents.

9. Avoid answering your own questions. If necessary, repeat or rephrase them until they are clearly understood. Or point out something you read in the leader's notes to clarify the context or meaning. An eager group quickly becomes passive and silent if they think the leader will do most of the talking.

10. Don't be afraid of silence. People may need time to think about the question before formulating their answers.

11. Don't be content with just one answer. Ask, "What do the rest of you think?" or "Anything else?" until several people have given answers to the question.

12. Acknowledge all contributions. Try to be affirming whenever possible. Never reject an answer. If it is clearly off-base, ask, "Which verse led you to that conclusion?" or again, "What do the rest of you think?"

13. Don't expect every answer to be addressed to you, even though this will probably happen at first. As group members become more at ease, they will begin to truly interact with each other. This is one sign of healthy discussion.

14. Don't be afraid of controversy. It can be very stimulating. If you don't resolve an issue completely, don't be frustrated. Move on and keep it in mind for later. A subsequent study may solve the problem.

15. Periodically summarize what the group has said about the passage. This helps to draw together the various ideas mentioned and gives continuity to the study. But don't preach.

16. At the end of the Bible discussion you may want to allow group members a time of quiet to work on an idea under "Now or Later." Then discuss what you experienced. Or you may want to encourage group members to work on these ideas between meetings. Give an opportunity during the session for people to talk about what they are learning.

17. Conclude your time together with conversational prayer, adapting the prayer suggestion at the end of the study to your group. Ask for God's help in following through on the commitments you've made.

18. End on time.

Many more suggestions and helps are found in *How to Lead a LifeGuide Bible Study*.

Components of Small Groups

A healthy small group should do more than study the Bible. There are four components to consider as you structure your time together.

Nurture. Small groups help us to grow in our knowledge and love of God. Bible study is the key to making this happen and is the foundation of your small group.

Community. Small groups are a great place to develop deep friendships with other Christians. Allow time for informal interaction before and after each study. Plan activities and games that will help you get to know each other. Spend time having fun together going on a picnic or cooking dinner together.

Worship and prayer. Your study will be enhanced by spending time praising God together in prayer or song. Pray for each other's needs and keep track of how God is answering prayer in your group. Ask God to help you to apply what you are learning in your study.

Outreach. Reaching out to others can be a practical way of applying what you are learning, and it will keep your group from becoming self-focused. Host a series of evangelistic discussions for your friends or neighbors. Clean up the yard of an elderly friend. Serve at a soup kitchen together, or spend a day working on a Habitat house.

Many more suggestions and helps in each of these areas are found in *Small Group Idea Book*. Information on building a small group can be found in *Small Group Leaders' Handbook* and *The Big Book on Small Groups* (both from InterVarsity Press). Reading through one of these books would be worth your time.

Study 1. To Us a Child Is Born: Isaiah's Prophecy. Isaiah 9:1-7.

Purpose: To refresh our hearts with this astonishing prediction of what God's coming King would be like and to ask what effect this will have in our lives.

General note. Consider beginning this study by playing a recording of the "Unto us a child is born" chorus from Handel's *Messiah*.

Question 1. Studying the map reveals that the region described includes upper and lower Galilee, the coastal plain and part of Transjordan, probably Gilead. Second Kings 15:29 shows that these areas had already fallen prey to the Assyrians before Ahaz's time. But in place of their gloom, distress and humiliation, and in place of their present condition, described only too accurately by the phrase "living in the land of the shadow of death," Isaiah predicts the dawning of a new and glorious day.

Question 3. The changes Isaiah predicts are glory for contempt (9:1), light for darkness (9:2), joy for sorrow (9:3), victory for defeat (9:4) and peace for war (9:5). In chapter 8 Assyrian strength seemed irresistible. But now there will be a wonderful victory like that of Gideon over Midian. The chafing yoke will be lifted, and the rod that beats them will be broken.

Question 4. Desperately looking for guidance, the people are turning to the spirits of the dead (necromancy) to learn about the future. Ahaz's political maneuverings have not been productive. As the awesome uncertainty of their position becomes increasingly plain, the people curse their king for getting them into this trouble and their God for not getting them out of it.

Question 5. The philosophy of history expressed by Isaiah is remarkable: even the most terrifying superpower of the age is an instrument in the hand of the Almighty God. We are not just in the grip of political and military forces that are beyond our control.

Question 7. These events did not take place in the time of any Old Testament monarch. But everything begins to fall into place when a descendant of David is baptized and anointed with the Spirit and begins to preach in Galilee that the kingdom of God has arrived—although he refuses to allow the crowd to make him a political king. As for the last phrase of 9:7, it contrasts with human zeal, which fades out all too quickly. When God becomes enthusiastic to bring something about, there is no force in the universe that can stop him.

Question 9. We live in a world in which God's bountiful resources are very unequally shared. This inequality is going to increase in the next twenty years because of massive population increases in the poorer countries. If those of us who are fortunate now do nothing or very little to bring about more justice and righteousness in the world, we will have reason to be nervous when God sets things right. But for those whose lives are a perpetual struggle for justice and righteousness, God's law and zeal will bring the peace we have been yearning for.

Question 10. The Wonderful Counselor encourages us when we are confused and distracted. The Mighty God is present when we are frightened and anxious. The Everlasting Father promises the hope of all eternity in the face of present difficulty. The Prince of Peace offers the lasting comfort we seek in a world of turmoil.

Now or Later. There are many possible answers. See for example John 1:46 and 7:52. Also consider the comments about Jesus' parentage, the saying that a prophet is not without honor except in his own country, and Pilate sending Jesus to Herod.

Study 2. Waiting and Hoping: Zechariah and the Angel.
Luke 1:1-25; 57-80.

Purpose: To deepen our faith that God always fulfills his purposes and promises, and that he uses people of hope and obedience to do this.

Question 1. Extrabiblical studies keep confirming the historical accuracy of the third Gospel. Luke's own introduction is in classic Greek literary style (1:1-4). He claims to follow the principles of good history: acquaintance with similar accounts, interviews with primary sources—eyewitnesses and leading characters—investigation of reported events, orderliness in arranging materials and a clear aim.

Question 3. This question is intended to get people to start looking at the text. Some possible reasons for God's choice: (1) They both descended from priests—their priestly pedigree was not a decisive factor, but this detailed emphasis indicates they knew and appreciated their rich spiritual heritage (v. 5). (2) They were "upright in the sight of God"—this does not mean they were morally perfect, but that their basic trust was in God's grace, not their own works. (3) They obeyed God's commands as best as they knew. (4) Zechariah had long been praying for the Messiah to come (v. 13).

Although Zechariah was a priest, he was one of "about eighteen thousand" according to Darrell Bock. And only once in his life would he have the opportunity to "assist in the daily offering by going into the holy place" (*Luke*, The IVP New Testa-

ment Commentary Series [Downers Grove, Ill.: InterVarsity
Press, 1994], p. 35).

Question 4. The angel is identified as Gabriel, a prominent angel in the Bible. He meets Zechariah in the house of God. His
message is specific and harmonizes with scriptural prophecy.
His message is for Israel and not a subjective situation. His
prophecy is objectively fulfilled.

Question 5. Why did Elizabeth go into seclusion? Scholars
aren't sure. Leon Morris notes that during the first five months
"her pregnancy would not have been noticeable. It may be that
she did not want to be seen until it was obvious to all that the
Lord had looked on her to *take away* her *reproach* (cf. Gn. 30:23).
Childlessness was usually considered a punishment from God,
and Elizabeth had evidently had to put up with reproaches
from people who did not recognize her piety (6). Now she would
know this no more." (*Luke*, Tyndale New Testament Commentaries [Downers Grove, Ill.: InterVarsity Press, 1988], p. 79).

Question 9. The birth of the Messiah's forerunner had to be
unmistakably God's doing. Consider their advanced age, Elizabeth's barrenness, the sign of Zechariah's muteness, the witness of many people to the effects of his vision in the temple,
the nine-month pregnancy itself, giving the name John ("gift of
God"). All pointed to the grace of God.

Luke loves to describe happy family/community scenes. Here
he starts this subtheme in his Gospel: people who witness or
participate in God's wondrous works naturally tell others about
it. But at this point Luke seems especially eager to give objec-
tive witness to this supernatural event.

Study 3. Nothing Is Impossible: Mary and the Angel.
Luke 1:26-56.

Purpose: To experience, alongside Mary, the joy and terror of being called and favored by God.

General note. If you have people in your group from a Roman

Catholic background, you should be familiar with the basic tenets of Catholic belief about Mary. Rather than engaging in long debates over the validity of Catholic teachings about Mary, a better approach will be to keep the focus of the discussion on what we can learn from the New Testament about Mary.

Question 1. Mary is traditionally pictured as a young woman, although no direct statement is made about her age. The normal betrothal age was fourteen, although a woman as young as twelve could be betrothed. The Jewish marriage process had two stages. In the betrothal period an agreement was made (usually between the fathers) that a man and a woman would marry. Often a financial exchange was also made as the bride's father paid the bride price or dowry to the groom or the groom's father. At this point the man and woman were legally betrothed. A divorce was required to break the agreement. The betrothal normally lasted one year, and it was during this time that Gabriel visited Mary. The second stage of the marriage process was the actual marriage ceremony, when the husband took his wife to his home, and the marriage was consummated through sexual union.

Question 2. God had used his Spirit and his Word to prepare Mary to be receptive to God's request, but Mary's "blessed" status was a gift bestowed by God.

The angel Gabriel appears four times in Scripture to men and women uniquely chosen and blessed by God. He always brings a significant message of hope for the people of God. Gabriel appeared twice to Daniel (Dan 8:15-19; 9:20-27); he appeared to an old priest named Zechariah to announce the birth of John the Baptizer (Lk 1:11-20); six months later he appeared to Mary.

Question 4. The name *Jesus* is the Greek form of the Hebrew name *Joshua* and it means "the Lord saves." The child's name summarized the whole purpose of his coming—to be our Savior. Gabriel's declaration that this child would be "the Son of the Most High" (v. 32) would have meant only one thing in Mary's Jewish mind. To say that someone was "the son" of someone else meant that the person had the same nature as the father. Mary's child would have the same inherent nature as God Most High.

Question 5. It seems that Mary believes what the angel says, but wants to know how such an event can occur. We have Mary's testimony before an angel of God that she is a virgin. Gabriel does not tell Mary specifically how she will conceive; he simply declares that God will do it! Our confidence in the fact of Jesus' conception in a virgin woman rests on the trustworthiness of the Scriptural record and the awesome ability of God to do what he promises to do. No "biological" explanation is possible; it was a supernatural act of God.

Question 7. Mary must have been encouraged and strengthened in her faith to hear of another work of God's power. Elizabeth had conceived in her old age, but she had conceived through her husband, Zechariah (Lk 1:5-25).

The exact relationship between Mary and Elizabeth is uncertain. Elizabeth belonged to the descendants of Aaron (Lk 1:5); Mary was from the tribe of Judah and the descendants of David (Lk 1:27). The word *relative* in Luke 1:36 is a broad term covering many possible relationships. We do know that Mary and Elizabeth knew each other well.

Elizabeth was given direct knowledge from the Holy Spirit that Mary was carrying the promised Messiah. The Spirit also in some mysterious way produced a response to the unborn child Jesus in the unborn child John and then revealed to Elizabeth the spiritual significance of her baby's leap in the womb.

Question 8. Mary's words are written in poetic form like an Old Testament psalm or hymn. Verses 46-55 are sometimes referred to as the Magnificat, because in the Latin version of the Bible (called the Vulgate) the first word of the poem is the Latin word *magnificat* ("glorifies").

Mary knew the Old Testament Scriptures. This poem is a series of quotations or allusions to Old Testament passages, most of them in the Psalms. A good reference Bible will direct you to more than twenty Scripture passages from which Mary draws her expressions of praise to God.

Mary also refers to the Lord at least eighteen times by name or with a pronoun. She sings back to God the wonderful aspects of his character that she has discovered in the Word of God and that she has learned in her personal experience.

Now or Later. This exercise provides an opportunity for creative expressions of praise to God. Depending on the talents and interests of the group, you may want to encourage instrumental music, vocal expressions, drama, poetry—any expressions of praise to God that come from a sincere desire to honor him.

Study 4. Divine Interruption: Joseph and the Angel. Matthew 1:18-25.

Purpose: To consider how we can respond appropriately to life's divine interruptions.

Question 2. Divorce was required to break the betrothal or engagement commitment. (See note for question 1 in study 3.) Because Joseph knew he was not the father of Mary's child, the only conclusion he could draw was that she had been unfaithful to him. In order to preserve his own reputation for righteousness, he knew he had to put her away. His love for Mary determined how he would do that.

The righteous standard of the law demanded that a woman who was unfaithful during the engagement period was to be stoned along with her male counterpart (Deut 22:23-24). Jewish tradition allowed an engaged husband to divorce his promised wife. In a public divorce, the man would charge the woman openly before a religious tribunal. The woman was shamed and disgraced in front of everyone. The alternative was a private divorce carried out before two or three witnesses. Joseph wrestled with the alternatives and finally decided that he would not publicly disgrace the woman he loved so much.

Question 5. God often allows us to come to the end of our wisdom and resources before he intervenes. Just when we think we have a situation all worked out or just when we are about to collapse, God acts to prove himself compassionate and wise. This testing of our faith produces patience—the willingness to trust God fully the next time we face a difficult situation. We *are* to think through hard decisions, but only after we have asked God to give us his wisdom (Jas 1:2-6).

Question 6. Several factors converge to demonstrate that this was a genuine message from God through an angel. First, Joseph had already settled on a decision to divorce Mary. He wasn't seeking some accommodation. Second, the angel's message confirmed Mary's account that the child was supernaturally conceived. Third, the angel's message was verified by an appeal to the prophetic Scriptures (vv. 22-23). Isaiah had predicted a miraculous conception of the Messiah.

Question 7. Mary had no way of defending her purity before Joseph. Mary's character was defended to Joseph by God's declaration through an angel; her character is defended before us by the reliable record of Scripture. If Jesus was born of an immoral relationship with another man or out of an unlawful relationship with Joseph, he was not God in human flesh, and the Bible (at least at this point) is a lie. The virgin conception of Jesus is not a biblical truth that can simply be ignored; it is part of the core of the Christian faith.

Question 9. Every major strand of biblical truth about Jesus is touched by the angelic message. Jesus would be supernaturally conceived (a unique being); he would carry out a saving work;

and he would be the visible presence of the invisible God—God with us.

Question 10. Not much more is said in Scripture about Joseph outside this passage. Sometimes a righteous person lives his or her whole life in relative obscurity. Joseph's quiet contribution to this marriage and home, however, laid a strong foundation for Jesus' spiritual and emotional development. We may be quietly used of God to help someone else do great things for God.

Study 5. Season of Wonder: Jesus' Birth. Luke 2:1-20.
Purpose: To experience afresh the wonder of the incarnation of God among us.

Question 1. Joseph would be taking the weeklong trip to Bethlehem by foot with Mary about to give birth to a baby that was not his. Mary would be feeling physically uncomfortable, deeply concerned for her unusual child and tempted to worry about the future. Then, once they arrive in crowded Bethlehem, there is no normal room in the inn, only space with the animals, possibly in the back of the inn.

Question 3. Luke has no need to embellish this awesome event. He lets the facts speak for themselves.

Question 4. Reflecting on the lowly and humble state of Jesus' birth can remind us of the values of God's kingdom—God is not interested in our material comfort but in our spiritual state.

Question 5. Moving about the country as they did, shepherds were known for thievery and unreliability. Moreover, other Jews despised them because they were unable to keep the laws on ceremonial cleanness. These particular shepherds, however, indicate some kind of Old Testament faith about the coming of the Christ. Still, to see and hear not one but a great company of angels makes the birth announcement personal and unforgettable for their witness to others. Social rejects are the first to hear of the birth of God's Son. Grace indeed! Luke's is a Gospel of grace.

Question 6. Verse 16 tells us that they "hurried" to Bethlehem, verse 17 says that they "spead the word," verse 18 reveals that all were "amazed," and verse 20 tells how they praised God for all they had seen and heard.

Question 7. They are trusting of God and one another. They are strong-willed, reflective and practical, realistic and hopeful. They are working together to fulfill God's will.

Study 6. In Search of the King: The Magi Meet Jesus. Matthew 2:1-18.

Purpose: To show that coming as the heavenly king, everyone must respond to Jesus. We either worship him or reject him.

Question 1. The contrasts between Jesus and Herod are striking. Jesus was completely Jewish; Herod was of a mixed race. Jesus was sent by God; Herod was placed on the throne by the Romans. Jesus was to be shepherd of Israel; Herod was an exploiter of Israel. Herod took the lives of children to keep his throne; Jesus gave up his life so that the throne might be given to him. Herod "occupied" the Jewish capitol; Jesus was born in King David's city.

Question 2. There are many legends about the Magi, in later church tradition they are even given names. Study of the ancient near-eastern culture suggests that they were astrologers who attempted to tell the future by looking at the stars. However, from this passage, there is not a great deal that we know about them. What is important to note is that these foreigners are able to find out about his birth and come to celebrate him, thus establishing that Jesus' birth has international significance.

Question 4. Help group members recall ways in which an interest in God has affected the books they have read, the friends they have chosen, the church they attend.

Question 5. People may have feelings of disappointment with God. This can be confusing because God's character is trust-

worthy. However, our expectations can lead us to expect God
to act in our behalf in ways that are not actually consistent with
his character. This leads to a feeling that God has let us down.
Question 6. Jesus is not welcomed by the established authorities of the Jewish world. He is welcomed by the foreign Magi.
The religious leaders did not seek out the place of Jesus' birth
and were not looking to welcome him.
Question 7. Herod was the first of many authority figures who
wished to put Jesus to death. Not being a full-blooded Jew, he
had reason to fear one "born King of the Jews."
Question 9. Someone once said that "God is obvious by his
absence and his silence is the loudest noise in the universe." In
this passage God is active in every single thing that happens,
but is seldom mentioned.

*Cindy Bunch is a senior editor at InterVarsity Press. She is also the author of the
LifeGuide® Bible Studies* Woman of God, God's Word *and* Christian Virtues.
She is the editor of Jesus' Final Week, *which is designed for use during the sea-
son of Lent.*

Sources

These studies are revised and adapted from the following Life-Guide® Bible Studies:

Study 1: *Isaiah,* Howard Peskett, revised edition, ©2001.

Study 2 and leader's notes in study 5: *Luke,* Ada Lum, revised edition, ©2001.

Studies 3 and 4: *Mary,* Doug and Karen Connelly ©1996. Currently out of print and used by permission of the authors.

Study 6: *Matthew,* Stephen and Jacalyn Eyre, revised edition, ©2000.

Look for these guides and other LifeGuide® Bible Studies online at www.ivpress.com or at your favorite Christian bookstore.

What Should We Study Next?

A good place to continue your study of Scripture would be with a book study. Many groups begin with a Gospel such as *Mark* (20 studies by Jim Hoover) or *John* (26 studies by Douglas Connelly). These guides are divided into two parts so that if twenty or twenty-six weeks seems like too much to do at once, the group can feel free to do half and take a break with another topic. Later you might want to come back to it. You might prefer to try a shorter letter. *Philippians* (9 studies by Donald Baker), *Ephesians* (11 studies by Andrew T. and Phyllis J. Le Peau) and *1 & 2 Timothy and Titus* (11 studies by Pete Sommer) are good options. If you want to vary your reading with an Old Testament book, consider *Ecclesiastes* (12 studies by Bill and Teresa Syrios) for a challenging and exciting study.

There are a number of interesting topical LifeGuide studies as well. Here are some options for filling three or four quarters of a year:

Basic Discipleship
Christian Beliefs, 12 studies by Stephen D. Eyre
Christian Character, 12 studies by Andrea Sterk & Peter Scazzero
Christian Disciplines, 12 studies by Andrea Sterk & Peter Scazzero
Evangelism, 12 studies by Rebecca Pippert & Ruth Siemens

Building Community
Fruit of the Spirit, 9 studies by Hazel Offner
Spiritual Gifts, 8 studies by R. Paul Stevens
Christian Community, 10 studies by Rob Suggs

Character Studies
David, 12 studies by Jack Kuhatschek
New Testament Characters, 10 studies by Carolyn Nystrom
Old Testament Characters, 12 studies by Peter Scazzero
Women of the Old Testament, 12 studies by Gladys Hunt

The Trinity
Meeting God, 12 studies by J. I. Packer
Meeting Jesus, 13 studies by Leighton Ford
Meeting the Spirit, 10 studies by Douglas Connelly

OTHER LIFEGUIDE® BIBLE STUDIES
BY CINDY BUNCH

Woman of God
God's Word
Christian Virtues
Jesus' Final Week, editor

LifeGuide® in Depth Bible Studies

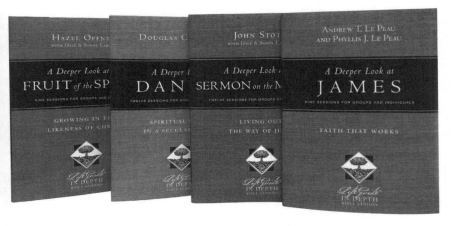

LifeGuide® in Depth Bible Studies help you to dive into the riches of Scripture by taking you further into themes and books than you might have gone before. As you see new connections between the Old and New Testament, gain an understanding of the historical and cultural background of passages, engage in creative exercises, and concretely apply what you've learned, you'll be amazed at the breadth of the knowledge and wisdom you gain and the transformation God can work in you as you meet him in his Word. Each session provides enough material for a week's worth of personal Scripture study along with a weekly group discussion guide that pulls all of the elements together.

These guides are based on and include the inductive Bible studies from the bestselling LifeGuide® Bible Study Series with over ten million copies sold. But they've been expanded for a new kind of study experience.